LinkedIn Publishing To Profits

A Simple 5-Step System to Attract High Paying Clients, Media Attention, & Speaking Engagements

Tracy Enos

#1 International Bestselling Author
& LinkedIn Expert Advisor

FREE Bonus Masterclass

This book includes step-by-step video training you can use RIGHT NOW to find and close high-end clients, paid speaking gigs, and media guest spots and posts!

No software, experience or list required! Get it NOW at
www.LinkedIntoPublishing.com

LinkedIn Publishing to Profits© 2018
Tracy Enos

For more information, please contact:
Tracy Enos at tracy@tracyenos.com

ISBN-13: 978-1-7320388-0-6

ISBN-10: 1-7320388-0-5

Table of Contents

FREE Bonus Masterclass

If you **want to Get 5-20 High Ticket Consulting Deals Each Month with Reliability & Predictability...**_Even If You've NEVER published before,_ **join me for a free masterclass:** www.LinkedIntoPublishing.com

Introduction

Welcome to LinkedIn Publishing to Profits!

This guide represents nearly four years of hard work, experience, and effort by my incredible team and clients. Maybe you're one of them!

Here is what you'll find in this book so you get the most out of it and meet your expectations.

First, it's interactive and short. It's packed with implementable content, ideas and opportunities for you to go deeper into the content, gain access to free training videos, participate in a free masterclass, and more. My intention, and the purpose of this book, is to show you a powerful way to market yourself, build a brand, generate qualified leads, close deals, and leverage the latest LinkedIn strategies to set yourself up for long-term growth.

Second, this book is for business. It's intended for implementers such as professionals, entrepreneurs, consultants, authors, and sales and marketing teams, to help you grow your business, produce qualified leads, and land that speaking gig or media interview.

You'll see there are LOTS of ideas that you can use to grow any business, in any industry, country, or language, anywhere in the world. All you need do is to set aside a couple of hours a week.

Third, If you're the type who's looking for the easy button, this isn't the book for you. In addition, this book is not for the person who wants to do overly promotional type posts or recruiters trying to post their jobs. This is for people and businesses who want to become the thought leader in their industries, showcase their expertise and authority, and provide true value to their prospects.

If you're not willing to do that, put in the work, or learn how to outsource this and still be a part of the process, then this book is not for you.

Fourth, this book wasn't intended as a be-all, know-all about LinkedIn. It's designed to start a conversation with you, give us a chance to get to know each other, develop trust, a relationship, and ultimately help us decide if we will work together in the future.

I'll be the first to admit, I have a helpful nature—and I want to help you reach more people, make more money, and add value to your life and everyone else you encounter.

Having said that, if you like what you read, *or most of what you read,* I'd love to hear from you, get to know you better, and have you post a success story or video on your LinkedIn Post or my inbox. Please tag me in LinkedIn using the @mention or send me a message if we're connected, or Inmail and connection request if we're not.
https://www.linkedin.com/in/tracyenos

Sincerely,

Tracy Enos, Kansas City, Missouri, USA

P.S. - I wrote this book myself in a very conversational tone, and was not ghostwritten. I don't consider myself a writer and most days allergic to it. This book was edited by my good friend and author, Michael Kravets, but not changed. If you find an error, do me a favor and tell me what you find by sending me an email to **tracy@tracyenos.com**. Just note the page number, sentence and mistake and I'll fix it right away. I'm all about results, implementation, and speed and I chose to give you tools that make you money over perfection. And like my mentor and friend, Mike Koenigs, once told me *"**Money loves speed and time kills deals!**"*

P.P.S. - If you love this book, found it useful, or make money, land a big media deal, or speaking gig because of it, will you please post a review on Amazon? If you DON'T like it, send me an email, tell me why and I'll give you your money back. Deal?

Please be kind. I have two teens still at home. They read what people say about me online and so do their friends. One of them has also joined my business. There's no sense in dragging an innocent kid into something unnecessary. Nobody likes a bully. Ok?

Endorsements and Accolades

"Tracy provided me an exceptional LinkedIn Site that has created a high number of leads and conversions. Her professionalism and knowledge of LinkedIn as well as other social media exceeded the value of my investment by at least 5 times. She also coached me to constantly improve my networking and marketing efforts and gave me GREAT advice on both. I am deeply indebted to Tracy for growing my business quickly!! Contact me any time if you want greater detail. You will not regret this investment in your business."
John Moore, CEO Moore Strength Executive Leadership

"I had the honor to meet Tracy via professional networking in 2012. Our fortuitous meeting has proved to be most beneficial to both of us in our respective professional endeavors. Tracy is a social media and marketing expert and practitioner. What sets Tracy apart from other such experts is the solid business experience, knowledge and wisdom she gained during her career before she began her present business venture. In short, this is a clear "difference maker" for Tracy in the competitive social media and marketing footprint. Tracy can practice her artful craft locally, regionally, domestically and globally with her network of experts across multiple industries and media platforms. Tracy is genuine, intelligent and competitive and she possesses the rare gift of intuition and common sense about business operations, sales and marketing. I greatly appreciate our growing collaboration on a number of business projects. I am most proud to give Tracy my *highest professional recommendation.*" **Bob Lovely, Executive Coach & LinkedIn Author**

"I met Tracy here on LinkedIn several months ago. Tracy has a deep understanding of Linkedin and how to gain the results companies are looking for off of the platform. We have had multiple meetings and in-depth strategy sessions recently giving my organization the clarity and expert consulting to raise the bar on the Linkedin. Tracy is attentive and detail oriented, straight forward no bull type of business person. I recommend her for all your platform marketing needs." **Dan McGowan, Green Net Solutions**

"Tracy is extremely knowledgeable in the areas of LinkedIn marketing and business development. I took part in a LinkedIn workshop that she hosted and was impressed with the depth of her understanding of social media and LinkedIn as a effective tool for branding and systematic lead generation. I would recommend Tracy to anyone who is looking for a hands on trainer and social media coach. Thank you Tracy!" **Ben Fromme, Bukaty Companies**

"Tracy, in my opinion, is the most outstanding social media expert I've ever met or worked with. She's been extremely helpful in improving my own LinkedIn profile. Not only has she provided invaluable insight for my LI profile, but has provided an endless variety of valuable coaching and advice in other areas relating to various other social media platforms I'm working with. Her skill sets in social media is broad and extensive. She's GREAT to work with and I simply can't recommend her highly enough! Using her

coaching services is bringing the results I'd hoped for! Don't wait...Call her today!!" **Randy Shephard, Ph.D, CEO Peak Performance Inc.**

"I recently attended two LinkedIn workshops led by Tracy Enos. I have had a LinkedIn account for years, but never utilized it to generate business. After Tracy's two day workshop, I had discovered tools and strategies on LinkedIn I never knew existed. I made 3 minor changes on my profile and within days had prospects reaching out to me to schedule meetings about my product. I highly recommend working with Tracy Enos to improve your LinkedIn results." **Justin Osburne, NIADA, Sarasota, Florida**

Foreword by Five-Time Best Seller Ed Rush

I'll get right to the point. If you want to get more leads, sales, and customers in a way that is fully brand-representative and flat-out excellent, then this book is for you.

I consider Tracy Enos one of the world's leading authorities on LinkedIn. In fact, for the last 3 years, she's been the brain (and brawn) behind my LinkedIn marketing funnel.

Here are some results:

When Tracy and I started working together, my account had a measly 260 connections and it hadn't been updated in 3 years. In a short 5 months, she added over 4,500 targeted connections and generated 400 leads coming through a landing page she helped me create.

Since then, I've had thousands more connections, been invited to speak in the Caribbean islands, and have attracted 5-figure consulting clients—all through the LinkedIn profile and plan that Tracy created for me.

The great news for you is Tracy isn't one of those "gurus" out there who teaches theory (or fluff). She's actually in the trenches marketing on LinkedIn every day. There are some people who DO and there are some people who TEACH. Tracy is the rare combination - a DO-ER of what she TEACHES.

I've run out of fingers and toes to count the number of people I have referred to Tracy. My guess is it's close to 30 people by now.

And I consider a referral the highest compliment I can give to any expert.

Here is what I suggest:

1. Read this book.
2. Implement what Tracy recommends.
3. And then smile. Your business is about to get a whole lot better.

Go do that now!

Ed Rush
Former F-18 Pilot
Five-Time #1 Best Selling Author

Tracy's LinkedIn Story

LinkedIn saved my life!

My LinkedIn story starts in October 2009. My born on date.

Now, LinkedIn was a place to create your online resume. It neither looked nor functioned like it does today. Back then you needed an invitation from a current member via email. Most of us ended up with two or more accounts. A violation of their TOS (terms of service).

I did nothing with my profile until February 2011.

By then I was ready. From 2008 until 2011 I had been laid off, got divorced, lost 18 pounds due to all the stress, and had health issues as a result. Also a myriad of other challenges reared up. But that story is for another book!

I had a friend in the real estate business, Michael Maher. I met him while I was living in Branson, when I was a loan officer at National City Bank. He was one of the coaches for company called Loan Toolbox. He did a short webinar back when webinars were getting started. They weren't as popular as they are today. He taught us how to use keywords in our profile to become visible in the first ten search results in LinkedIn.

Back in 2011, that was a whole lot easier to do than it is today. I implemented his information and I found a job listing that seemed interesting. I updated my profile to his suggestions and answered the ad. A phone interview later and I was hired.

I started as a promoter and within a couple of months became the regional manager's assistant. Then a couple of months later, I became the field regional manager. I was in charge of seven states and 83 Costcos and Sam's Clubs recruiting and training new promoters. We used a combination of Craigslist and LinkedIn to find talented staff.

I spent a lot of time traveling and evenings alone in my hotel room.

After long days and chatting with my kids, I would spend the rest of my evenings immersed in LinkedIn. I took some online courses implementing what I learned. And often taught my friends and colleagues how to use the platform for free.

I had 60 connections in June 2012. I wanted to grow my connections, but went about it the wrong way at first. I did what everybody else did back then: I tried to get as many connections as possible. I would connect with anyone and everyone. "Social proof," they said! I followed advice from a program I purchased. It had a database you could download and they would accept the invitation to connect with you. Unfortunately not everyone did. And, many of them complained to LinkedIn that they did not know me.

Within a few weeks, I got suspended from LinkedIn. This was back in the day when LinkedIn actually sent an email. Good luck getting one today! Anyway, they sent me an email describing why I got suspended and how long. I got suspended for connecting with people I didn't know, for 5 days, and if it occurred again it would be 2 weeks. A third offense was permanent removal.

Then I got laid off in November 2012. I had only been with my current company 8 months.

With no idea of what was next for me and living off savings, I continued to dive into LinkedIn. This is when I met Bob Lovely, on LinkedIn. You'll get to read and hear his story later in the book.

He is a master at publishing and has made a full time income with a part time effort.

That's when I really started using LinkedIn to find new connections. And, I did it without automation tools. By the end of 2012, I had around 1,200 connections. Good, targeted connections. People whom I knew or wanted to do business with.

The following February, I received an email from LinkedIn. It stated I was in the top 1% of all LinkedIn profiles for the year 2012. They had 187 million members. I felt proud to have been given that honor. Currently I am still in top 1% of my connections and people in my industry. This started my career with LinkedIn.

Still not sure what I was going to do, and running out of savings, I traveled to San Jose. My sister, Terri, was suffering from terminal brain cancer. This would be the last time I saw her before she passed.

She too had started a corporate career and left to start her own successful design business. Over a few glasses of wine she advised me to start my own business. I had started a side gig while working with SGN Nutrition, but wasn't charging people. She encouraged me with her kind words and years of experience. I came home and launched my boutique marketing agency.

I found my clients using my existing network and attending several local networking events. Each week I would attend several meetings. It was a lot of work, time away from my kids, it was expensive, and clients only trickled in. So, I turned to LinkedIn.

I started getting most of my clients through LinkedIn in 2013.

Over time my clients started asking me how I was doing it, and they wanted to learn how. This is when I started writing and charging to optimize and update profiles.

Like many of you reading this, I subscribe to a lot of influencers' newsletters. One person I followed was Mike Koenigs. I had been following him for years, and though I was never a customer, I was on the email list. I *always* read his emails.

One email described a marketing event he was holding in September 2014. It was my birthday weekend, so I treated myself by attending the event. The first morning of the event they had us fill out a questionnaire if we wanted to be selected for one of the *hot seats*. I was chosen the first day. And, in 7 minutes the panel dissected my business. The panel included Mike, Ed Rush, Pam

Hendrickson, and Paul Colligan. In those seven minutes, they encouraged me to fire all my clients, write a book and coach people to use LinkedIn. I took heed of their advice. I came home, finished up a couple of clients, fired another one for nonpayment, and the rest is history. Well, sort of!

It wasn't as easy as it sounded. I didn't know how to market my coaching and consulting services. I had already been doing a lot of done-for-you services. I created profiles for people and business owners, and did some light marketing. At first, I started teaching for free. I was a volunteer with SCORE.org, a nationwide nonprofit. I conducted Constant Contact and LinkedIn seminars for them. This is how people were discovering me, and the coaching business was born.

Business was doing well until the Spring of 2015.

It started out on Good Friday. I, yes me, did something very stupid. I was cleaning out my garden and I have a loose rock in my planter. I was wearing flip flops and stepped off using the loose rock. What resulted was a four-stage ankle sprain, no good. That following Sunday, Easter Sunday, my boxer dog all a sudden couldn't walk. He's was 70 lbs. He hurt a disc in his back playing in the backyard. I didn't know how I was to pick him up and no one was home. It took an act of adrenaline and his willpower to get back into the house. The next day he was prescribed prednisone and stayed on it until his passing.

The following June, my uncle passed away. I would travel to Kansas City as a child from California every summer to visit him. What great memories I have.

Days later my computer got hacked. I fell for a phone scam. You know the one, "It's Microsoft calling and I understand you're having a problem with your computer." I fell for it. Hook. Line. Sinker. I was actually looking for help online because I was having a problem with my computer. They knew. That error cost me hours reinstalling my operating system and creating coaching materials. Moral: Microsoft doesn't call you!

Then on July 7th, 5:30 in the morning, I suffered from the most horrific accident.

I was making a pot of brown rice pasta for the week. The noodles were done, the colander in the sink, resting on top of some dishes.

The pot was overfilled, I was barefoot, and I didn't want to spill the hot water on my feet. So, instead I moved out of the way because it was spilling. While I making sure not to burn my feet, the pot was already in motion. Forward motion and I didn't want to dump everything on the floor. I tried to pour it into the colander, the colander tipped and it all came back on me. Pasta and hot boiling water. I started to scream bloody murder, my boyfriend runs down stairs, picks me up and throws me in an ice-cold shower. Clothes and all!

About 20 minutes later, I got dressed in dry clothes and head the emergency room. They did what they could to cut away the dead skin, wrapped me up and sent me home. A few days later I was referred to the burn unit.

My appointment was on Tuesday morning. My left arm had 3rd degree burns from my armpit to my elbow and my right arm and hand were 2nd degree burns. My son Asher, now 17 (he was 15 at the time), came with me. He was crying because of how much pain I was in as they were cleaning up the dead skin on my arm.

What developed after that appointment was six days in the burn unit. I was only supposed to spend three but the damage was worse than they initially thought.

My second day in the burn unit, they convinced me to try hyperbaric oxygen therapy. Anybody know what a hyperbaric oxygen therapy is? It is a well-established *treatment* for decompression sickness, a hazard of scuba diving. Currently it's a popular treatment for burn victims. It enhances the body's natural healing process by inhalation of 100% oxygen in a total body chamber, where atmospheric pressure is increased and controlled.

I have never been able to scuba dive. I cannot equalize my ears past 13 feet. I have no problem flying, however.

So I'm scared to death to get in this hyperbaric chamber. I get swimmers ear easily and hearing is the one sense that I treasure most.

Finally convinced, I get in the hyperbaric chamber and it dives down to 23 feet and takes 45 minutes. I got to watch some TV, drink some of my water. I was pretty doped up on morphine, so I was kind of happy. I survived treatment, everything's fine. I wake up the following morning at 2 AM and I can't hear. I flipped a lid. I went ballistic. My heart rate went to 112 beats per minute. My resting heart rate is in the 60's.

Now, there's only six beds in this burn unit, everybody's asleep and there's one nurse on the floor. She is doing everything that she can to get me to calm down, but my blood pressure keeps going up.

She gets an emergency room doctor to come in and shoot me up with a bunch of more drugs and Lorazepam. An anti-anxiety drug.I have never experienced this type of anxiety before. I was scared.

It was pretty traumatic what I went through. I ended up having five surgeries in nine months. I wore a compression sleeve for a year. I also contracted MRSA while I was in the hospital. I ended up with depression, anxiety, and gained over 50 pounds, I hibernated. I sat behind my computer all day. I made any excuse not to engage with my kids or clients outside of my home.

For the sake of this story not getting any longer than it is, I will tell you this. Had I not created a foundation and a system in LinkedIn, my business would not have survived. I would have gotten evicted and my car repossessed. Homeless.

Had it not been for LinkedIn, I would have not generated any new business while recuperating. While in the hospital I generated over $3,000 in new coaching business. And, in the following 60 days, generated another $6,000 in coaching fees, and $3,000 in done-for-you services. My article was featured in LinkedIn Pulse and went viral. This is the premise of the book and how to do just that.

I have gone from charging $300 per client to over $5,000 per client in a few short years. All because of LinkedIn, a $97 training program, some persistence, and a system.

LinkedIn saved my life!

What is Linkedin Publisher

Per LinkedIn, LinkedIn Influencer was designed to designate approximately five hundred professionals as Influencers. They were invited to publish on LinkedIn by LinkedIn. This was a secret club and you had to apply in order to become an influencer. Some people were automatically given this status such as well known corporate CEO's and business moguls like Richard Branson, Arianna Huffington, and Bill Gates.

These influencers would publish articles about corporate leadership, hiring, any company disruption, firing practices, business best practices, and how to succeed. LinkedIn closed Influencer in 2013, but they selected a few regular members to become beta testers of their publishing platform—what has become LinkedIn Publisher today.

I was one of those selected back in 2013, and I did nothing with it. Zero, zip, zilch. But I started talking to people I knew about it. I don't always drink my own Kool Aid. Shame on me for not taking advantage. I missed out on a huge opportunity to gain an edge over my competition. I will have a case study later on in this book about my friend Bob Lovely, who I encouraged to start writing.

In early spring of 2014, LinkedIn rolled it out to all the members. Bob jumped on the bandwagon in June of 2014. He has written an article religiously every single week. Every Tuesday morning, he hits the publish button without fail. I didn't publish my first article until August. It was a press release. It was terrible. Terrible. I published my first *real* article in September of 2014, and that article was indexed on page one of Google for its keywords until last year. It was awesome! So why am I not publishing an article every single month? Did I mention I don't always drink my own Kool Aid? But when I do, it's powerful. It's because I have created a process, a system. Read on.

Let's distinguish some of the vocabulary and timelines, because it can be confusing.

Publisher is the platform where you create your articles. It is also commonly called a *Long Form Post.* These articles live on your personal profile.

A Short Form Post is a 1300 word mini-story that posts directly to the Home news feed. These feeds are what you see when you first log in to LinkedIn.

LinkedIn Pulse was active up until midyear 2017. LinkedIn removed Pulse and its Pulse Channels. This was where you could follow all the channels that you wanted and LinkedIn would send you featured articles that other members had written. For example, my October 2015 article on productivity was featured in the *LinkedIn Tips* channel.

This was the article that generated me 3 new high end coaching clients in a few days.

Today it's the "What People Are Talking About Now" feature on the right of the desktop home screen and the home screen of your smartphone app. According to LinkedIn, "The stories you see in your feed under the label **What people are talking about now**, are the top professional news and conversations of the day. These stories are surfaced to help you stay informed about topics that colleagues, partners, peers, and other members may be talking about today. These topics are selected and curated by our news editors, leveraging data on and off LinkedIn."

LinkedIn also sends you a "Daily Rundown" notification each morning in your Notification tab of hashtags and articles that are trending. If you have not turned off your Daily Rundown notification, you will also receive an email to your primary address each week.

To get featured in **What people are talking about now** can be challenging, but you don't need that exposure to leverage the publisher platform successfully.

The Facts about LinkedIn Publishing Today

According to LinkedIn's 2017 *Sophisticated Guide to Content Marketing*, nearly 2 million unique writers publish more than 130,000 posts a week. About 45% of readers are in the upper ranks of their industries: Managers, VPs, and CEOs.

Don't let these facts deter you from writing and publishing.

Do it right

There is a specific strategy if you want to improve your chances of LinkedIn taking notice. Do this right and you can start generating leads and media and speaking gigs overnight, even without LinkedIn's help. I promise you; I've done it. I have clients that have done it. You don't need thousands of people liking and viewing your post in order to generate leads and interest. If you've targeted your audience, have a great profile, an article with a compelling headline, story and message, you're bound to win.

In the coming pages I'm going to give you some strategies and my system. However, it's not an exact science. Even the editor of LinkedIn mentioned in one of his articles that there's not an exact science to this. Not every article is going to get picked up, your profile will constantly be improving, and LinkedIn WILL create new features and remove others.

Should I or my business publish on Linkedin?

The short answer? Yes!

There is a LOT of money in publishing.

Good content has the power to completely transform a business. If a business is just starting out, it can put that business on the map.

If a business is slowly dying on the vine, good content can turn that business around.

Are competitors giving you problems? Well, you know the answer – you are just one article away from leaving your competitors in your dust.

In fact, I like to say that the answer to every business problem is GOOD, VALUABLE CONTENT.

So when you start to think about putting a few extra percent (or more) onto the bottom line of just about any business in the WORLD... well you can start to understand when I tell you that we are talking about an a GREAT DEAL of money.

If you have that power – the power to write **content that positions you as the thought leader and authority**, well you can start to understand just how powerful that position is.

With all that money riding on good copy, is it any wonder that there is a huge mystique around it? And a HUGE amount of misinformation.

This is the deal – there is a saying that I learned from Dan Kennedy... he says:

"Beware The Wizard."

By that, Dan means that you really have to watch out WHO you learn from. If you are going to spend your time and money to learn a business skill, you have to make sure that the person you are learning from is teaching from EXPERIENCE.

You also have to make sure that they actually have the skill to teach what they do. There are folks who write great content, but they don't have a clue how to share that skill in a way that anyone can understand.

Even worse are those wizards who conspire to keep you begging for table scraps.

Believe me, the results might LOOK like magic – but LinkedIn Publishing is a skill, and it's a skill that you can learn.

In fact, it's...

The One Skill That You Absolutely Need

Here is the thing – no matter where you are in your business, writing is the one skill that you absolutely need.

And it's the one skill that you really shouldn't outsource (but you CAN!)

If you are just starting out – maybe you are a one-person shop – then you NEED to be able to write content. You probably can't afford a top-notch writer. And even if you can afford to get your content written by someone else, you will still need to know enough to evaluate that content.

On the other hand, maybe you have a larger business with a staff. You know the only way to leverage is to outsource almost everything to employees and contractors. HOWEVER, you can't outsource your marketing and your content.

I mean, you can have someone WRITE your content – but you need to have enough writing skills to be able to hire the right person and evaluate that content.

No matter what your writing skills, I have been there too…

Like I said above, 4 years ago I had never heard of LinkedIn Publishing. So if you are a newbie with writing, I can vividly remember what it was like… all very confusing at first.

But then I remember the incredible feeling of power when I wrote my first piece of content… and it started to pull RESULTS!

It was like I had the keys to the kingdom at last.

I had just learned a skill that enabled me to create cash-flow on demand… whether I was promoting my product or service, helping one of my clients promote theirs, gaining media attention, or getting paid to speak.

You can learn this skill just as easily as I did. And you can feel that same incredible power when you learn how to write words that get people to send you money.

Street Cred… Those "3 New Clients" Worth Thousands From One LinkedIn Publisher Article I Wrote

Of course, if I had stayed there, at that newbie beginner level, then you wouldn't be reading this book right now…

But I didn't—I kept at it, working at copy and studying—and now I have more people approaching me to coach them than I could ever help individually. And they are paying me good sums of money when I can fit them into my schedule.

Now you might think this is a remarkable story – to go from beginner to top of the heap in a relatively short period of time… but that's really not what this book is about.

My goal here is to convince you that publishing is something that YOU need, and it's something that is well within your grasp.

Will this work in my market?

You have an inherent advantage in your market, simply because you are more familiar with it.

So if you take your knowledge of your specific market and your specific prospects, and you learn to create good content (it doesn't have to be GREAT content... even good content will completely CRUSH your competition), then you have the recipe for big-time LinkedIn Publishing success.

You don't need that superhuman content that the Gurus and Influencers keep rubbing in your face (and shoving down your throat).

If you have content that sells and you mix it with knowledge of your market and solutions to pain-points, then you have a winning combination that you can literally take to the bank.

While this works best for B2B (business to business), we are seeing a growing trend of B2C (business to customer) companies using the platform for branding and business development.

Is it Free to Use Publisher?

One of the very few things left in LinkedIn that is free regardless of whether you're an unpaid or premium member is publishing an article. However, I cannot guarantee that this will be free forever. In 2017, once the Microsoft acquisition was finalized, I saw the most platform changes than I had seen in any one year. My advice: get on the publishing bandwagon before LinkedIn makes you have to pay for it.

How to access Publisher

The best way to access Publisher is through your desktop, laptop, or a tablet device with a keyboard. It is extremely difficult to create a Publisher post from your phone.

Log in to LinkedIn. It's going to take you to your Home page.

At the top and middle of the page, you will see a "Write an Article" button. Click on it and it will take you to a new screen where you can start creating your content.

The new publisher dashboard will allow your save and see your existing drafts, start a new article, or see your published articles. Click the down arrow in the top right corner to access any of these options.

Now that you know how to access Publisher, I'll bet you just can't wait to dive right in. And I'm sure you're expecting me to tell you how; and I will. But really the whole point to using Publisher is to get people to see your *profile*. It was my Publisher article that got picked up by LinkedIn Pulse and went viral that helped generate five figures in income while I was recovering from the burns. The article led them to my profile, the one I had spent so much time tweaking, and it was my profile that helped me close those sales.

So before I show you how to research and write your posts, I'm going to show you why your profile is so important, and then lead you point by point in making your profile the best it can be. By following these profile pointers, you'll skip over the trial-and-error phase I went through and start creating a profile that will start converting your readers into customers.

Why is my profile so important?

In nearly a decade since I have been on Linkedin, the platform has grown from 187 million to over 550 million members. What was once a place to add your online resume has now morphed into the largest professional networking platform of its kind. And to many it's still a mystery how to use it. The belief is that it's still a place to add your online resume and find a job. While this is true in part, most businesses still treat it this way and not as a sales and marketing tool.

99% of all your activities in LinkedIn are tied to your personal profile. Your profile photo, your name, and your headline are typically what someone will see first.

This is your first impression, and if well done will compel a member to visit your profile.

Below are some activities and how its tied to your profile.

Requesting connections

There are two ways to request a connection. Using the canned message or customizing the invitation. I suggest you do the latter, ALWAYS! Either way many members will take the opportunity to view your profile before accepting your request. If your strategy was to be selective who you are targeting, you have one chance to make a great impression.

Posts (short form)

These are the posts you seen when you log in to your home page. When you post a video, a short story, a business success, or share your content or someone else's, LinkedIn will share with a small portion of your network.

The first thing they will see is your photo, your name, and your headline. If your network engages with your content (or post) their network gets notified. It's six degrees of separation and can make your content go viral.

I had a post that went viral in February of 2016. This post generated 5,500 profile views.

Google

Ever Google yourself? We find that your profile is indexed on page one for most people when their name is searched. Usually your LinkedIn profile will show up before your website and other social media. Google will show a bit of information from your profile.

Articles

Additionally, if your publisher posts are done well they too will be indexed by Google on page one for its keywords. When someone finds your article they will see your information below the headline as the author.

People researching you

LinkedIn members are often looking for prospects and others to help them in their businesses. When a search is done in the main LinkedIn or in Sales Navigator, members will see your name, photo, and headline.

Groups

Getting active in groups? You should!

Groups were dying (or died in my opinion) until recent news. LinkedIn has now decided, starting in 2018, to post your discussions and videos from the group into the newsfeed. Again, as the authorof these posts, your network will see the same information as the other posts.

Company pages

Currently company pages are limited in features. However, that is set to change in 2018. I am not sure of the new features or when they will roll out, but today if you follow a company page and engage, the admins and other followers of said page will see your name, photo, and headline.

So, hopefully you can see how important it is to have a well done profile. Your activities and engagement in LinkedIn depend on it.

In the next section, we will talk about how to identify your prospect and build a compelling profile.

Step 1: Position

Identify Your Target Audience

The first step in writing your profiles and articles is to Identify Your Audience. Too often I see profiles and articles that are written for their industry and not to their ideal client or customer.

You must know your prospect intimately. If you want to consistently attract your ideal customers, you need in-depth knowledge of who they are, their deepest fears, pain points, and what keeps them up at night. Without this knowledge, you'll waste hours trying to figure this out. I call this Hope Marketing. I stole that term from master marketer, Jeff Walker. Hope marketing is when you throw something at the wall and you hope that it sticks.

Take a moment to think through exactly who it is you want to target. Who is your ideal customer or client? If you answered "everybody", "any business owner" or "every U.S. based sales executive", that's NOT the right answer.

Get the picture?! If all you can come up with is the above, take a closer look at your clients right now. Think about the types of people you really like working with and are your best clients from a financial perspective. Now it's time to build a real prospect profile.

There are two types of data to consider: demographics and psychographics.

Demographics are statistical data relating to the population and particular groups within it. Or, in other words, intelligent information about your target customer.

Some questions you might answer:

- What are your target industries?
- What geographical area are you targeting?
- Are your prospects most likely to be hanging out in certain LinkedIn Groups?
- What company size is the right fit for you? A one-man shop? Only companies with more than 50 employees?
- What types of position titles does your buyer usually hold? Come up with the top 10 to 15 positions that you target.
- What level of annual revenue do your best clients have?
- Are they married, divorced, or single? Kids?
- Men or Women?
- Age range?

The Sales Navigator tool also has many filters to help you define your target demographics.

Some of the filters are above and some others include:
- Groups
- Function
- Years in position
- Company
- Company headcount

- Years of experience

HINT: Think like your prospect. Your search is only as good as what someone adds to their profile. For example, if you're prospect is a CEO, he might abbreviate his title or spell it out (chief executive officer). If your prospect is a business owner they might have the title of owner, co-owner, president, or CEO.

Psychographics is the classification of people according to their attitudes, aspirations, and other psychological criteria, especially in market research. Or, in other words, how people think and their current state of mind.

Some questions you might answer are:

- What are the biggest challenges your ideal client faces as it relates to [x]?
- What are the top three things that keep them up at night?
- What types of products or services [in this area] have they already tried? What did they like or dislike?
- What factors do they consider when purchasing a product or service?
- What are their top 3 goals as it relates to [x]?
- What are their profound opinions as it relates to [x]?
- Where do they stand politically or religiously?
- How do they feel about [current trends, news, etc.]
- What publications do they read and subscribe to? Online and offline.

- What's their business language? (Hint: not your industry speak)

Now, you want to take this information, and build a quick cheat sheet that you can easily refer to.

There is a really cool tool that I use from HubSpot. I love HubSpot. They offer great resources, like this one, for free. It's MakeMyPersona.com. You can either create it online by answering about twenty questions, or you can download it as a PowerPoint or a Keynote file. This is great if you have more than one type of buyer, or one type of prospect, you can create multiple personas.

Interviewing Your Past Clients

Having problems answering the above questions? If you can't understand your current customers, you won't understand how to attract your next customers. So you won't get leads and sales.

If you've been in business for a few years a shortcut is to get on the phone. Call your past clients and interview them. Ask them the above probing questions.

TIP: Look at your top accounts from the past 3-5 years. This will give you historically which accounts have been the best.

Bonus - Interview Questions

This worksheet includes step-by-step questions you can use RIGHT NOW to discover how and why your clients hired you!
Get it NOW at
www.LinkedIntoPublishing.com

Keyword Research

This is the backbone of how your profile will be found organically in search. This is also not to be confused with keyword research for creating articles, however they do overlap some.

For those of you new to this concept, let's define what keyword research is.

Keyword research is a practice professionals use to find and research search terms that people might enter into search engines for topics, people who provide that service, or information to help them solve a problem. Once a niche keyword is found, it can expanded on to find similar or variations of those keywords.

Google is the most common search engine used today. However, what most people don't realize is that although it's not as robust as Google, LinkedIn is a fantastic place to search for your target audience.

Does your LinkedIn profile show up in search results?

Think like your prospects. What search terms might they type in to find a product or service you provide? You can get some great intel from LinkedIn by just typing keywords into the search bar. Start by brainstorming a list of up to 50 search terms. Terms or keywords your audience would type in to find your products or services. Keywords can be broadly or narrowly defined.

You will use these key terms in your profile. By adding these keywords to your profile it will improve your chances of you showing up in someone's search results organically.

Here's a simplified example of keyword phrase brainstorm for marketing to dentists (this is not a complete example):

Defined Industries (non-franchise): pediatric dentist, pediatric orthodontist, cosmetic dentistry, endodontist, periodontist

Title: owner, ceo, chief executive officer, partner, co-owner, founder, president

Pain Points: team productivity, client retention, repeat clients, referrals, performance management, customer service improvement, employee headaches, staff development, etc.

Brainstorming Keywords: staff development, dental staff development, team building, patient attraction, business development, dental development, patient retention, dental patient retention, team building.

The above is not a full brainstorming session, but hopefully you get the idea.

TIP: Research other professionals in your space. Check their websites, LinkedIn profiles and company pages, social media, and so on. This will not only help you stay on top of your competitors but help you find additional keywords, pain points, and viral topics.

LinkedIn search also works with Boolean search. **Boolean search** is a type of **search** allowing users to combine keywords with modifiers such as AND, NOT and OR to further produce more relevant results.

According to LinkedIn Help, here are some ways you can construct your Boolean searches:

1. **Quoted searches** - For an exact phrase, enclose the phrase in quotation marks. For example: type "product manager".

2. **NOT searches** - To exclude a particular term, type that term with an uppercase NOT immediately before it. For example, type: programmer NOT manager.

3. **OR searches** - To see results that include one or more terms in a list, separate the terms with an uppercase OR. For example, type "sales OR marketing".

4. **AND searches** - To get results that include two or more terms in a list, you can use the uppercase word AND as a separator. For example, type: manager AND director.

5. **Parenthetical searches** - To do a complex search, you can combine terms using parentheses. For example, to find people who have "VP" in their profiles, but you want to exclude "assistant to VP" or SVPs, type VP NOT(assistant OR SVP)

Link: https://www.linkedin.com/help/linkedin/answer/75814/using-boolean-search-on-linkedin?lang=en

How Do I Create a Profile That Speaks To My Audience - Part 1

In the above chapter we discussed that your profile can be discovered by a prospect through a relevant keyword search. The next step is to optimize your profile in a way that shares your subject matter expertise, tells a compelling story filled with benefits, and encourages a prospect to engage with you and your articles. This is not a book about profile optimization (I could write a whole book on that subject), but rather an overview to help you get started.

To begin we will start with what a prospect might see above the fold when landing on your profile. We are assuming you're on a laptop or desktop.

Above the fold is an old newspaper term. They printed the best headlines on the upper half of the paper to encourage you to purchase it. It's similar with your profile. Your background photo, name, and headline are the upper half of your full profile.

Profile Photo

A good profile photo speaks volumes and gets 14 times more views than not having a photo at all. I've seen the photos of people with booze in their hand, on vacation, with their dog, and their logo. You want your photo to convey professionalism.

First, choose a photo that looks like you. I know this sounds elementary. Have you ever met someone and they don't look like their photo because the photo was taken 20 years ago? If so, would you question their credibility?

Choose a photo that was taken in the last couple years.

For a good profile photo, my recommendation is to have a neutral background showing your head and shoulders, and smiling. No glamour shots or selfies in the car. I too am guilty of taking selfies in the car and they're a lot of fun, but I don't post that on my profile.

Don't have a photo? Nowadays you don't need to go to a professional portrait studio to get a good photo. If you have a smartphone with a good camera and some great lighting, that's all you need.

TIP: If you want to brand yourself across all social media, use the same photo everywhere you have an account.

Background Photo

Background photos used to be for premium members only. However, as of early 2017 it became available to all members. This is prime real estate and I see many members not taking advantage of it.

The LinkedIn profile cover photo is 1584 pixels wide by 396 pixels high. This is exactly 4:1 proportion and can be repositioned if the photo is too large or small.

It can be pretty tricky to create on on your own. Some of my favorite tools are Canva, YouZign, and hiring a graphics designer on Fiverr. For $25 you can get a great photo done for you.

Now you might be asking what should the photo include. In the last 4 years of creating various designs for clients, they all have something in common. That one thing is a CTA or call to action. This could be a phone number, website address, landing page, podcast, link to their book, etc.

The best practice is to brand it to your company and website. However, for the price of $25 from Fiverr, you could easily change it to reflect your current focus. I do this often depending on who I am targeting and what my offering is.

My suggestion is to look at some backgrounds in LinkedIn to get your creative juices flowing.

Some of my favorites as of this writing are:

1. Keith Lee: https://www.linkedin.com/in/keithlee-1/
2. Charles Martin: https://www.linkedin.com/in/charleymartin/
3. Damien Baden: https://www.linkedin.com/in/damien-baden/

4. Michael Cielenski: https://www.linkedin.com/in/michael-cielenski/

Name

Best practice is use your full name. Refrain from using emojis and first name, last initial. However, I understand that we are in an emoji world. And, in my opinion, it's unprofessional. Save it for Instagram.

If you have credentials such as M.D., Ph.D., O.D., or Dr., and you are comfortable adding those to your name, it's respected and will further create trust and credibility.

Headline

How many of you reading this have a headline that states, "CEO at XYZ Company?" or "VP of Marketing at ABC Company?" Your profile shouldn't read like a resume and nor should your headline. It should be about what you do and who you do it for, rather than what you are.

This is where we start to reverse engineer a profile that will showcase expertise, who it is that you help, the benefits and outcomes of working with you, and what separates you from your competition.

Use your prospects' language—language they can understand. If they are not familiar with your industry, company jargon, or internal language they may move on to the next profile. It won't matter how great your headline is if they don't understand the wording.

More recently there are certain adjectives that are off putting to some. Instead of adding adjectives such as expert, hard-working, best, or superior use a benefit statement of prior success.

Example: "Helped 40 Pediatric Dental Practices Increase Client Retention by 30% in 2017"

Headlines can get tricky. With only 120 characters you must get creative. When working with my clients, I suggest they brainstorm 5-10 possible headlines. Make sure you customize it to your audience (which pre-qualifies the prospect), include your USP or value proposition, use their industry specific language, and refrain from exaggeration. Also, try adding your keyword(s).

Another tip is to write your headline in title case. Title case is capitalizing the first letter of each word. Words such as to, for, and, can be left lowercase. This make it easier to read online and on mobile.

There are many different ways to craft a great headline. Let me share a few examples to get you started.

1. Tired of Dental Practice Overwhelm and Frustration? Get More New Patients. Make More Money. Master Your Practice

2. Training and Coaching Leaders to Become Highly Influential—The Key to Steady and Sustained Business Growth

3. Custom Digital Marketing to Build Trust, Drive Results via Inbound & Outbound—Specializing in Agriculture, Food, and Energy

4. Creating Inbound Marketing Campaigns that Deliver Continuous Solutions to Help Turn Leads into Customers & Drive Results

5. Helping Sales Managers Keep Their Employees Engaged and Productive

6. Helping SaaS Startups Get Results on Social Media

The upside to crafting a great headline is you'll start noticing a difference in the quantity and quality of leads you generate on LinkedIn.

How Do I Create a Profile That Speaks To My Audience - Part 2

This is the part where we start adding the core information to your profile. In this chapter I will cover how to craft a compelling Summary, Experience (current position), and Skills.

Summary

"Tracy, how do I create a compelling Summary that is client centric and shows off my and my company's expertise?"

I get this question often.

There are no right ways to create one, however there are a couple DO NOT do's.

One mistake I see that many make is that their Summary still reads like a resume and it's often done in third person. You must understand that this is a *personal profile* and not your resume or company page. It's not about you. The prospect wants to know *WIIFM* or "What's in it for me" if I hire you.

Have you ever heard of someone talk about themselves in third person? Did you get annoyed? I know I sure do. It reflects one's perception of himself or herself as being larger-than-life.

About a year ago I was taking my now 17 year old son to his cheerleading practice. I don't remember exactly what were chatting about. We were sitting at a red light I said, "Yeah, Tracy this, and Tracy that." He looked at me and he goes, "You're annoying." I'm thinking this is teenager speak, right? I'm like, "What are you talking about?" He says, "You're talking about yourself in third person. It's annoying." I went, "Oh, I really was. I'm so sorry."

People like to do business with others they know they can trust. What you want to do is humanize your summary. You want to edify yourself somewhat, but not to a point where it's all about you. The summary isn't all about you, all your successes, or how smart you are.

Here's a formula for writing a quick Summary:

1. **CTA:** Add a call to action in the first two lines. LinkedIn truncates your summary on both mobile and desktop. Tell your prospect what you want them to do next. Some ideas may include sending them to your website, book a meeting on your calendar, landing page, email or phone. *The Summary sits behind a click, so it is essential to use the first 2 lines to position yourself and inspire the viewer to click 'See More...'*

2. **Share a little bit about you and your experience:** Humanize yourself. If you're comfortable, talk about previous experience, about your family, how you got where you are today.

3. **Tell them what you do:** This is your current focus. Explain what you and your company does.

4. **Who you do it for:** In a prior chapter I covered how to find your ideal prospect. This is who you do it for. You must spell it out to pre-qualify those who reach out to you.

5. **What you do for them:** Share in a couple sentences what product or service you deliver and how you do it.

6. **Outcomes:** What can they expect the outcomes to be if they hired you.

7. **What separates you from the competition:** Take the high road here. Without blatantly bashing your competitors, explain what your product or service does that separates you. You identify features, benefits, and solutions that would solve a particular problem they are facing in their business.

TIPS:

- **Summary is 2000 characters:** Write your profile in a Word or Google doc. Write a rough draft and then refine. Trying to write in LinkedIn or from your mobile device is very difficult to do. A better option is to copy and paste your description in the Summary. I once had a workshop attendee try to accomplish this from his phone while I was teaching. I commend him for trying, and he came up to me later and told me that it wasn't the easiest to accomplish.

- **Write short paragraphs:** Over 54% of all members will access your profile from a mobile device. LinkedIn uses light grey as its font color. In itself it's hard to read. If you write with chunky paragraphs, similar to a white paper, most won't read it. Try writing no more than 2-4 sentences.

- **Use unicode symbols and headings:** LinkedIn doesn't allow you to add unicode symbols (such as bullets) if you're writing directly in LinkedIn. By copying and pasting your description you can add unicode symbols to your copy ahead of time. This helps break up the content for both those linear reader and those that skim copy.

- **Use a testimonial:** Nothing edifies you more than a great testimonial. People have been conditioned to read reviews online. Try adding a heading such as "What Others Say" and then add your testimonial.

- **Keywords:** DON'T forget to add your keywords conversationally in your Summary. Remember this is how you will improve your chances of showing up in search.

- **Media:** Add your videos, images, Slideshare. Use keywords in the headline and add a keyword rich description.

Experience

The Experience section is typically where most people would add their past and current positions or their jobs in a resume style. We're going to reverse engineer it.

It too is similar to the Summary. This section is limited to 2,000 characters, using keywords, and further defining your products or services.

Headline

Most would put their current title or position, such as CEO or Managing Partner, or VP of Sales at XYZ Company.

You're going to make a benefit statement rich with keywords. If you're adamant about adding your title, then do so after your statement. You get 100 characters to work with.

Here some examples of some client's headlines:
- Dental Practice Staff Development - Consulting Dentists Worldwide
- Helping Medical Companies Sell and/or Acquire ANDA's or NDA's
- Gazelles Business Growth Advisor for Dentists and Professionals | Founder, Speaker, Author

Location

Instead of adding where your company operates, try adding a CTA, website, or where you work geographically.

For example, if you're located in Kansas City, MO but operate worldwide you could create this:

Worldwide | Schedule Your Breakthrough Session at www.TracyEnos.com

Description

How do you reverse engineer your current position?

Instead of treating your company and your position like a resume you will want to create a miniature sales page. Sell them on your products and services. Remember the formula: Feature + Benefits + Outcomes = WIIFM.

A shortcut to this formula is using your website as a tool. You don't need to reinvent the wheel. Many company websites are well done and include many of your keywords.

Here is a great example of one of my client's current positions. I took it directly from his website.

Visit Us: https://www.newwestern.com/

✓ NWA serves 13 Major Metro areas nationwide
✓ Has sold 10,000 + investment properties
✓ Over 1 Billion in Real Estate Transactions
✓ Proprietary New Western Comp System

New Western Acquisitions (NWA) is a real estate brokerage firm. It was founded in August 2008 with a goal to acquire and resell distressed residential property for its affiliated holding companies. The company started in Dallas, TX and moved into the entire DFW market, Houston, and San Antonio by the end of 2010.

Since then, New Western has grown nationwide expanding throughout California, Georgia, Pennsylvania, Colorado, Tennessee and Florida. When originally conceived, the company placed an emphasis on dealing exclusively with real estate investors; thus enabling it to create a unique brokerage style and create its own niche market.

WHY CHOOSE US?

New Western's clients focus the majority of their efforts on reselling, renting and seller financing property to achieve the greatest possible ROI. Every associate who works for New Western Acquisitions is a licensed real estate agent (or broker) and receives in-depth training on the full scope of residential property investments above and beyond the state education requirements.

WHAT'S YOUR INVESTMENT PROPERTY WORTH?
https://www.newwesterncomps.com/ - You can generate a full, in-depth CMA report on your next potential investment, giving you the information you need to make the best decisions!

We have brought together some of the most advanced algorithms and user-friendly technology to compare the numbers you care about most. In seconds, this exclusive system allows you to customize, save or print detailed data of your desired property and its neighborhood comparisons, while also previewing your possible returns with a multitude of financial calculators.

Search for Your Next Investment Property TODAY!
http://www.NewWestern.com

TIPS:

- **Have more than one product or service?** Add another current position within the same company. Use a different headline and CTA. Add relevant media to that particular service.

- **See the Summary tips:** They apply to this section too.

- **Use Title Case in your headline:** Title case is where you capitalize the first letter of each major word for ease of reading. Prepositions (e.g., to, for, by), conjunctions (and, but), and articles (a, an, the) are not capitalized, except at the beginning of the line.

- **Past Positions:** If your past experience is relevant to your current industry, make sure you add relevant keywords to enhance profile visibility. Any other past experience can be listed like a resume. Add your successes and how you benefited the company in the description.

- **Create your company page:** In order for your logo to show up you must create a company page and upload a photo. To create, login into your profile, click the *Work* grid, scroll to the bottom and click *Create a Company Page.* Follow the prompts to create.

Skills

In an earlier chapter I discussed how to brainstorm 20-50 keywords. Along with adding these terms to your other sections, it's vital to add them here, too. Add up to 50 skills using keywords that relate to the problems you solve for your ideal clients, particularly skills to be endorsed for.

Your goal over time is to get each of your skill endorsed 99+ times. Not only is this social proof, but it will improve your chances of getting found in search.

Choose 3 to feature in the beginning. These should be your most important keywords. Then as your skills reach 99+ endorsements, rearrange them accordingly to encourage others to endorse.

Having trouble getting 50 skills?

Here's a quick example how I can make this one keyword into 3 : Social Media Marketing
1. Social Media Marketing
2. Social Media
3. Marketing

TIPS:

● Use Title Case for ease of reading and professionalism

How Do I Create a Profile That Speaks To My Audience - Part 3

Early in 2017 LinkedIn redesigned the entire desktop UI (user interface). The *Accomplishments* section groups together supporting achievements, information, and showcases your human side. These include projects, publications, organizations, courses, languages, certifications, and honors and awards.

I am going to give you the fine points of each and some ideas on how to reverse engineer each section.

Projects

List any relevant projects to support your expertise.
Here are some ideas:

- Current or past client successes: Showcase your expertise by sharing the feature + benefit + outcome and transformation of a client.
- Add podcasts, speaking gigs
- Past and current workshops or seminars (online or offline)
- Add your evergreen webinars
- Add longer testimonials

TIPS:

- Use Headline formula (as seen in Experience section); 255 characters
- Use Title Case in headline
- Use Keywords in headline and description
- Add a URL if possible
- Add a contributor: Must be first connections to add
- Add up to 2,000 characters in description
- Add a date

Publications

Share recent publications relevant to your expertise that you wish to drive traffic to.

Here are some ideas:

- Add podcasts or speaking gigs
- Showcase your articles (online or offline)
- Add your guest interviews
- Showcase your book
- Add a URL

TIPS: See Projects

Organizations

This section is where you can add some of your human side. By doing this you are creating the know, like, trust factor. Many times I know when someone has read my profile because they will mention certain items that they liked in their message. This is an ice breaker.

Add organizations that you belong to or support. Make sure you add your title (e.g. board member, donate annually, etc.) and a short description. Grab a description about the organization from their website.

Courses

I believe this section was created for the college grad, however I like to reverse engineer it. If you have too many projects already, you might choose to add your online courses or your sales funnel in this section instead.

Languages

This is self-explanatory. If you are proficient in any other language, add it here. LinkedIn gives you options to choose your proficiency.

Certifications

List any ~~relevant~~ certifications relevant to your past or present industry.

Honors and Awards

Use this section to create a list of accolades. Make sure you add a detailed description.
Some ideas include:

- Your best selling book (NYT, Wall Street, or Amazon)
- Collegiate awards
- Honorary member
- Sports awards
- Certification of appreciation

How Do I Create a Profile That Speaks To My Audience - Part 4

As you can see in the previous chapters, creating a client centric profile is the most important piece before publishing. It's also important to complete the profile. These last 4 sections will complete the profile. Additionally these tips will help you get found by Google and improve your chances of getting found in LinkedIn search.

Volunteer

Similar to the Organizations section, people want to see the human side of you. They want to get to know you, be able to trust you.

Add the organization name, your role, date, and a short description about the organization and your role.

For example, in my profile I volunteer at SCORE. They are a nationwide non-profit that help existing businesses and those looking to start one. Instead of stating that I am just a volunteer, I created the role of "LinkedIn Workshops & Social Media Mentor."

I then added a description about who Score is and those they serve. Their website is a wealth of information. I just grabbed some copy and pasted into this section and added a bit about how I volunteer.

Remember to use your keywords in these sections if your role is relevant to your current focus.

Education

It's important to add any secondary education to this section. Sometimes people want to do business with those that attended or graduated from the same school. Emphasize your academic history. Along with the name of your school and degree, include any achievements, such as a high GPA or any academic awards.

If you did not graduate from a traditional college but have education elsewhere, add it. I never finished college, however I have enough credits for an Associates. I did not add my college experience, but instead added other education I received. This included the U.S. Navy and MREC (Missouri Real Estate Commission).

On occasion I come across a profile with "Jack of all trades" or "School at Self." In my opinion this is unprofessional and not the best practice. If you don't have education, leave blank, however most of us have some sort of continuing education with our current or past jobs.

Contact Information

Did you know that Google crawls your business information all over the web? If you want to get found in Google search for all your social and business directories add your company info. Make sure that it matches your website.

For example, if you abbreviate your street name in one directory and spell it out in another, Google may not associate it with your business. The key here is to be consistent in how you format your address and phone number.

123 Southwest Street, Ste. 102 vs. 123 SW St., #102

A great place to check your address and is endorsed by Google is USPS.com.

Websites

LinkedIn allows you to add 3 websites on your profile. This is an advanced tip, and your competitors are probably not doing this.

Instead of using the canned options, choose *Other.* Add your keywords for the description, and the URL you want to send prospects to. You can add your other social profiles, certain pages on your website, your landing page, etc.

Some Examples:
- International CEO Consultant
- Develop Your Dental Staff
- Free LinkedIn Training
- Like Us on Facebook

TIPS:

- Use Title Case
- Title is only 30 characters. Get creative.

Recommendations

According to LinkedIn, they recommend members having at least 10 recommendations on their profile. Why? Because, like online reviews, they show people your expertise and trustworthiness. Your recommendations could be the one thing that makes your prospect reach out to you. In addition, this is a great strategy to use to help with profile visibility.

When asking for a recommendation from someone, LinkedIn allows you to include a personalized message with your request.

Instead of using the canned message, "Hi Ed, can you write me a recommendation?",
create a template and ask them to use your keywords for that service you provided. Most people aren't great at writing, so ~~by~~ providing a template is helpful.

Here's ours:
Hi Ben! Thank you so much for being a valued client. I hope you found our workshop and additional training helpful.

As you might know recommendations are an integral part of LinkedIn's search. It, too, is keyword driven. If you found our

56

services to be worthy of a testimonial, would you please recommend me/us?

If so, please use keywords for the service we provided, such as "Dental Workshop" or "Dental Consulting."

Thank you in advance,
Charles Smith

If you have been working on your profile as you read along with Step 1, you should now have a profile that ROCKS! It should make your prospects *eager* to call you and become your customers. The next step is to get them to engage with your profile, and you'll do *that* through Publisher. But before you start drafting your posts, you'll need to do the background work and research to find topics that interest your target market. And that's what Step 2 is all about.

Step 2: Prepare

What Makes A Great Publisher Post?

You don't need to be a guru or a LinkedIn Influencer to write well. You have undoubtedly seen examples of some amazing articles. And, they may have deterred you from attempting to write and publish for yourself or your company.

But, guess what? In your market you probably don't need amazing articles. If your content is 50% as good as the guru or influencer's content, then you're going to clean up and crush your competition.

Let me tell you, it isn't very hard to get your content 50% as good as that guru or influencer's content. Your copy doesn't need to be perfect, you just need to follow a basic formula. You don't need to turn content into art, you just need it to sell.

One more piece of advice: your content is good enough! So many times I have coached consulting clients that keep going over a piece of content time after time, they keep tweaking it and changing, and working on it but they never get it out on LinkedIn Publisher. I will tell you this, if you never finish your article and publish it, you will never make any sales. It is better to get a piece that is 80% right out in the market than have a piece that is 99% right that you never publish. Good is good enough.

Research

Before you think about writing a post you need to do some research. In 2014-2016 LinkedIn made it easy. They published an editorial calendar with a specific topic and hashtag to use. This no longer exists. Anyway, October 2015 was productivity hack month. This was my first article using the calendar. I wrote about Linkedin's and Evernote's partnership. This partnership was no secret. It had been out for a while, but it was still unknown to most.

Within 24 hours of writing that post, not only was I featured in Linkedin's Productivity Pulse Channel, it's generated over 2,300 views, over 5,500 profile views, 200+ new connection request, and 3 new clients. All in 2 hours of work. Here's the fun part. Most of the content was not mine. I just had my story with the content, how I found out about Evernote, and Dotto Tech's videos on how to use it. And, my article was indexed on page one of Google for its keywords for 2 years beating out Richard Branson's productivity article.

Read the article here: https://www.linkedin.com/pulse/linkedin-productivityhacks-why-i-love-evernote-you-should-tracy-enos/

Topic research in LinkedIn is simple. Login and navigate to the search bar. Type the keyword phrase you want to search for, hit enter, and click on *Content.* Additionally, if you have Sales Navigator, there is a search filter for *Posts.*

Remember to use some simple Boolean search operators if your search query is not netting you the right results. Putting double quotes around a keyword will net you an exact search (e.g. "digital marketing"), while not adding the quotes will give you a broad search (e.g. digital, marketing, digital marketing.)

Sometimes this is a great opportunity for you to see what your competitors are writing about, or what's trending in the industry today. If you hit writer's block, this is great way to get your creative juices flowing. When you're searching for posts or articles, you may want to also try using a hashtag. However, for now hashtag searches are only accessible using the mobile app.

Topic Research

In the last few paragraphs I mentioned how to find engaging and trending content using only LinkedIn. A great way to keep track of your brainstorming sessions is to create a spreadsheet, Google doc, or use a whiteboard.

Here are some additional free and cheap resources to start brainstorming and researching your topics.

Your Emails

Just this past week I had a client struggling to find topics to write about. He had never written a blog post or article before. I asked him if he had ever received an email from a client with a problem or obstacle? And, had he provided a solution?

By asking this question, he had a light bulb moment, and in the first week shared two articles with me. Both were amazing for him never having written before.

The first article was about how device distractions (notifications from apps on mobile devices) are ruining your productivity. He took inspiration from a video post by Ed Rush, and and article I wrote. This is called content curation. I will talk about this in the next chapter.

The second, a story about a specific client that had been with him for years, got impatient, and went to a big box retailer to upgrade the plan. It was a nightmare and he almost lost a client due to the store's negligence.

The moral here is to find those emails from clients and prospects with problems and obstacles. No doubt you responded with solutions. Create articles with a storyline and a solution.

Current & Past Client Interviews

In a previous chapter I talked about interviewing your past clients to build your prospect profile. If you took me up on my bonus, you should have received a document with those questions. You will use these questions to find your customers' pain and motivation. These questions have been tested to produce the best responses. The wrong questions will lead you to misunderstand your customers. And, if you can't understand your current customers, you won't understand how to attract your next customers.

Take your answers and brainstorm a list of potential topics to write about.

10x10 Formula

I learned this from a very intelligent, successful, and charismatic marketer, Mike Koenigs. This formula is also great for creating LinkedIn native videos in the newsfeed (short form posts.)

Here is how the formula works:

1. Write down the top ten frequently asked questions about your product or service.
2. Write down the top ten questions a potential prospect SHOULD be asking you about your product or service. These are the important things that differentiate you from your competitors and tap in to the experience, skills, and knowledge that you've acquired over your career.
3. Record 20 short Q&A videos asking and answering each of the questions you wrote in steps 1 and 2. Each Q&A video should be 30 seconds to 5 minutes long.
4. Transcribe videos to use in your articles or news feed posts.

For Example:

- If you're a digital marketer, it might be, "answers the most important   questions you should ask before hiring a digital marketing agency."
- If you're a dentist, it might be, "answers the most important questions you should ask before getting ANY cosmetic dental work done."

Repurpose Content

When it comes to marketing shortcuts, this is one of my favorite. You've done the hard work, let's reap the rewards.

When repurposing content, you create a piece once and use it in many different ways. That means less work and more results. It seems too good to be true, but I promise you it's not.

Let's look at a few ideas on how you can use your content and create great articles.

- **SlideShare or PowerPoint:** Did you or your company create a SlideShare or PowerPoint presentation? Take these talking points and use them as inspiration for articles.
- **Speaking Gigs:** In October 2017 I spoke at a GKIC's Info-Summit. It was recorded. I took that recording and got it transcribed. This gave me some inspiration to help me write this book. It's also a great way to get your articles written quickly.

- **Webinars:** Have a successful webinar? Similar to speaking, you've put in the hard work to create a successful presentation. Transcribe it and write!

- **Videos:** Created videos about your company, company culture, trending topics, video testimonials, other content? If it's relevant to your audience, get these transcribed and use as inspiration.

- **Blog Posts:** Repurpose your website blogs and publish in LinkedIn. Make sure you add a link back to your website. Google doesn't consider this duplicate content and won't penalize you.

- **Podcasts:** Take your video or audio podcasts and create content out of them. Get them transcribed and add a link to your original podcast.

- **New Content Out of Old:** Sometimes old posts may not be relevant today. But, with a bit of an update they can be. Create a new title, update the facts or strategies, add more content. To read more about this strategy follow Buffer's Kevan Lee. https://blog.bufferapp.com/repurposing-content-guide

BuzzSumo

BuzzSumo is powerful online tool that allows any user to find out what content is popular by topic or on any website. They have both free and paid options. The free version is very limited and the paid option is a bit pricey, but well worth the investment. Use the free option to simply type in a topic or domain and the site will net results over the past year on what types of content are performing best amongst all social platforms.

For our purposes, Buzzsumo is best used for content research, finding influencers, and brainstorming headline formulas that work.

Feedly

I love this tool! For a mere $65 per year you can find trending and up-to-date articles on any subject matter. I use this for inspiration for both long form and short form posts. Similar to BuzzSumo, Feedly will share the popularity of an article.

If you completed your prospect profile and defined their psychographics, you should have come up with some online publications they follow. Simply plug these into the search and in seconds the most recent articles will appear. You may also type in a keyword or topic.

Additionally, you can save these publications into feeds or segmented lists.

Google Alerts

Want to go the free route? You can set up alerts in Google for your topics and competitors. Google will then email you on a daily or weekly basis.
Feedly also works with Google Keyword Alerts.

Google Trends & Insights

Google Trends allows you to explore a multitude of topics, what's trending now and how it's trending geographically. I have been playing around with this tool and added several topics to my spreadsheet that I wouldn't have thought of initially.

To access: https://trends.google.com/trends/

Searcher Intent

Up until a few months ago I was teaching my clients how to use keyword research to create their content. My strategy changed when I read an article by SEO and marketing expert, Neil Patel.

LinkedIn is considered an authority site and your articles have a good chance of getting indexed by Google. With Google keeping webmasters and SEO companies on their toes and making changes often, I want to give you a few reasons why writing articles based on keyword research shouldn't be the main focus of your time and efforts.

1. Keywords are extremely competitive, even long-tail ones. It can take hours to find a non-competitive one even with the best tools.
2. Research is a waste of time because top-ranking posts aren't targeting the "quality content marketing" keyword. Google has changed it's algorithm (again!)

3. Keywords for articles force you to write outside of your comfort zone. Nothing worse than having to do a ton of research on an unfamiliar topic.

4. No matter how great of a keyword you find, if you don't have the best content, people won't consume it and you won't get engagement. People who know their stuff write the most profound content. They have a niche. They know their audience.

5. Your content should be geared toward your niche.

Here's some things we should be focusing on instead.

According to Neil, we should focus on *searcher intent*. We should be focusing the fulfilling the needs, wants, and desires of our core audience.

So, how do you focus on more searcher intent?

Think about your topic, then conduct a search in Google.

Let's say for example I wanted to write about "Linkedin vs Facebook." I conducted a search to see what other companies have determined intent to be.

I come up with this:

● Facebook vs. LinkedIn - What's the Difference? - Forbes
● Facebook vs. LinkedIn: Which One is the B2B Marketing Winner ..

- LinkedIn Vs. Facebook: Which is Better For Business Networking
- The Battle of Social Media Advertising: Facebook vs. LinkedIn
- LinkedIn vs. Facebook for Professionals: A Social-Media Smackdown

This shares with me that someone wants to know what's best for their marketing efforts, and which will likely produce better leads for business.

In the past we would use tools such as Google Keyword Planner or other keyword research tools. Today we should concentrating on writing the best content we can. But, remember as I stated in a previous chapter, you don't need to write like those gurus or Influencers.

Next, in your search you should check out Google's topic suggestions.

Here are my results:

People also ask

What is the difference between Facebook and LinkedIn?
What is LinkedIn and Facebook?
What is a LinkedIn profile?
How do linkedin make money?

This is fantastic because Google just suggested some additional ideas on what people are searching for.

As you can see, content keyword research should be replaced with searching for searcher intent. Once you have done this basic search, you are ready to start crafting your publisher post.

More tips: https://neilpatel.com/blog/stop-keyword-research-for-blogging/

Now, let's go write real content for real people!

Step 3: Publish

Starting in 2017, all long and short form posts became public and can be seen in the news feed, on your profile, and by search. By writing great content you have the potential to grow your network exponentially.

The Reader's Path

The reader's path is something even the "experts" miss. Your readers will take different paths through your published article, in fact, they will have almost an infinite number of paths through your content but there are 2 paths that your copy absolutely must be written for.

Some of your prospects will read the entire article straight through from top to bottom; this is the easy one that most people write for. However, many authors, even some of the gurus, completely forget about the skimmers. Depending on your marketing, your message, the skimmers might represent the majority of your readers. The skimmers will glance over your copy quickly moving through various sections. Sometimes they will immediately go to the end and read the call to action and then go back and breeze through the article.

You need to write for both the linear readers and the skimmers. If you don't you will kill your response. Remember that 54% of all LinkedIn members access their publisher through a smartphone or a tablet. If you can hook both types of readers, you'll have a better chance of engagement and conversion.

What's The Best Formula for Writing?

The formula for writing a great post is not a finite one. In the following paragraphs I am going to give you some great tips to get you started. Once you are consistent writing your articles, you should analyze each and start creating more content based on popular topics and engagement from your network. LinkedIn did away with the most of their analytics in 2016, so my suggestion is to create a spreadsheet and add your articles and their performance.

Types of Posts

According to data provided by BuzzSumo, posts that perform better follow the 5 P's.

- Personal
- Professional
- Practical
- Portray a path for change
- Point toward peak experiences

In another study conducted by Noah Kagan at OkDork and Paul Shapiro at Search Wilderness. They analyzed over 3,000 LinkedIn publisher posts. The types of posts that worked best are:

- How to's
- Listicles or List-Style

They also mention that question post don't work well; however, I have seen viral posts with this type of headline.

I have found that posts that combine a story, pain point, and solution draw in more people than plain how to's or list type posts.

Remember I covered how to dive into the psychographics of your prospect? Take this information and apply it to your articles, if possible. If you don't have a personal story, borrow one, or create one using your interviews. Emotion draws people in. They are driven by pain, desire, and outcome.

Length

Between 2012 and January 2017, BuzzSumo analyzed over 228,000 Pulse articles. According to the research, articles between 1,000 and 3,000 words were shared the most on LinkedIn.

Now, I am not saying that you have to write a 3000 word article every time, however in my experience, they do perform better.

My last two articles (May and February 2017) were long articles.

As a test I decided to create between 2000 and 3300 words. What happened was nothing short of amazing. These articles performed better than my last few that were around 800-1000 words, netting me new business, a paid speaking gig, and a feature article in Funnel Magazine.

Can an article be too long? That depends on your audience. One of my clients, John Moore, wrote his first article in September 2016. He is a 30 year Army veteran and a highly sought after military trainer. His first draft was well over 3000 words and read like a white paper. With a little tweaking, it was condensed to around 2000 words. In less than 24 hours he was approached by a popular military trade journal and asked if they could re-publish his article. Additionally, he secured new coaching clients with little effort.

Takeaway: Test your articles. What works for others may not work for you. And, not every article will be a homerun.

http://contentmarketinginstitute.com/2017/03/linkedin-publishing-sharing-trends/

Photo

The first two items that a potential reader might see is your photo and headline. These items are what will compel a reader to open and consume your content.

LinkedIn allows you to display your photo in the center or full width of the article. I prefer centering it.

To add a cover image: Click the area above the article's headline.

For best results images should be 744x400 pixels

Add photo credits by clicking into the text field **Add credit and caption**, located below the image. Example: Credit: 123rf.com

TIP: If you created your own photos, try adding a CTA or your website in the credit section.

Your photo should reflect what the article is about. I like to purchase stock photos so I don't run the risk of a copyright infringement lawsuit. My favorite sites are 123rf.com and DepositPhotos.com. Choose the medium size.

Refrain from using Google Images for the simple reason that you run the risk of choosing a copyrighted image. If your use of that image is found by the owner or copyright holder, you may get slapped with a copyright infringement lawsuit, or at least a "cease and desist" letter or email.

Several years ago, my friend Derral Eves shared with us a story. This was before he became Mr. YouTube. He was in the local marketing space. He had an attorney client in Florida. He was working with him marketing five of his offices. He used a photo that he purchased from another stock photo site (not 123rf), and got slapped with a $4,000 copyright infringement lawsuit. The settlement came out of his pocket and not his clients.

Another idea is finding photos on creative commons sites like Unsplash and Flickr. No photo credit is needed, but I am sure it would be appreciated.

If you want to add more pizzazz to your photos, try using free sites like Canva.com or BeFunky.com. Personalize it further with your logo for branding.

Art of the Headline

The headline has never been as important as it is today. A well thought out headline cuts through all the noise and grabs someone's attention. They also should evoke interest, emotion, deliver on a promise, or be benefit driven.

Your headline is the single most important part of your article. If you blow it here, then the rest of your article can be pure gold and it won't matter, because it won't compel someone to read it. Spend at least 80% of your time brainstorming your headline.

How do you craft a great headline? You don't have to be the most experienced writer or a great copywriter to model after those before you.

First, you must do your topic research. Next you will want to brainstorm 5-10 headlines per article.

Research confirms that a headline in LinkedIn gets more readers if it 40-49 characters. If it's any longer the headline gets truncated. We have tested both, and if you plan on not promoting your article, then stick with the shorter headlines.

In the above section, I referred to how to articles and list type articles that work best. These are not the only successful headlines that work.

Here are some tried and tested formulas that work. These work outside of LinkedIn too for blogs, email subject lines, etc.

HOW

Formula: How to Recover From a [Common Problem Keyword]
Example: How to Recover From an **IRS Audit**
Formula: How to [common industry task] Like a Pro
Example: How to **Create a Facebook Cover Photo** Like a Pro

LIST-TYPE

Formula: 5 [Industry] Books You Need to Read
Example: 5 **Social Media Marketing Books** You Need to Read
Formula: 25 [Blank] Hacks: A Cheat Sheet for [Blank]
Example: 25 **LinkedIn** Hacks: A Cheat Sheet for **Viral News Feed Posts**

WHY/WHAT

Formula: What Everybody Ought to Know About [Niche Keyword]

Example: What Everybody Ought to Know About **Cryptocurrencies**

Formula: Why [Common Industry Problem Keyword] is Killing Your Business

Example: Why **Not Hiring Overqualified IT Managers** is Killing Your Business

Now it's your turn:

- How to [benefit] in [period of time]
- How to Use [blank] to [benefit]
- What Kind of [blank] Are You?
- Which of These [blank] Should You Use?
- [blank] 5 Reasons You'll Love...
- Why [famous person] Is Wrong: [blank]
- WARNING: [potential mistake or threat]

My friend and client, Ed Rush, wrote anand article in 2017 that created a lot of buzz. It's based on a topic he knows well, being a fighter pilot. He used his experience to teach a business lesson. It follows the same headline formulas I mentioned above.

Ed's Headline: **"How to Fight & Beat MiG-29 (And Still Make it Home For Dinner!)"**

Need Some Additional Inspiration?

The above formulas are very simple and great to get you started. But sometimes you want to create more complex, controversial, or newsworthy headlines. Check out some of these sites to gain more inspiration.

Upworthy

Many of these headlines can be outrageous. Browsing this site will help in brainstorming catchier titles.

Google Images

Ever been in line at the grocery store and picked up or purchased a magazine? Do you know why the store puts them there? Because the headlines jump out at you making some sort of promise, celebrity tragedy, or outrageous claim that you can't help but buy it. It's definitely an impulse buy, and that's the point, isn't it?

Don't want to buy a bunch of magazines? I learned this trick from my new client, Damien Baden. Grab some inspiration by logging into Google and type in the search bar: [Name] magazine cover > Click on Images.

Example: Enquirer Magazine Cover > Click on Images

You can see on the covers of these magazines headlines that are geared to grab attention, evoke emotion, make a promise, or are benefit driven.

Upworthy Generator

These are fake titles and a bit outrageous, but they will certainly get your creative juices flowing.

Body

Before you start writing your article in Publisher, I have a couple tips.

TIP: Consider writing your rough draft in another program such as Google Docs or Word. Why? First, you don't own LinkedIn. If they were to go offline tomorrow (highly unlikely) or you got banned permanently, ~~youryou're~~ content is gone. We talked about repurposing in an earlier chapter and you may want to use your content on your blog, repost in Medium.com, or Quora, etc.

TIP: You can save your drafts in Publisher. However, the options for formatting are limited. If written first in another software you can use different heading, bullet styles, etc. Then copy and paste into publisher and do some light editing.

Let's get started!

As you write your rough draft, keep in mind how your readers will access your content. Whether they read it on mobile, desktop, or laptop, LinkedIn's font color is grey. This makes it a bit hard to read. Best practice is to not write it a white paper manner. You know those stuffy, long paragraph, technical papers. You want your audience to be able to consume your content quickly and engage.

According to some new research by OkDork, you should write your content in a neutral tone. I have to disagree with that data somewhat. Write conversationally and put your personality behind your writing. I feel that articles that have a storyline which addresses a problem and a solution is what is working best now. If it happens to be a bit controversial, so much the better.

QUICK TIPS:

- Write in short 2-4 sentence paragraphs
- Use headings to break up thoughts and flow
- Use topic keywords and keyword phrases conversationally in article
- Use bullets points where relevant
- Write for a 7th grade level. You want the masses to understand your content.
- Use the Hemingway app to help you write http://www.hemingwayapp.com
- Break up the content with a quote: Highlight your quote and click on the quotation mark in the editing bar

Media

Many of the most engaged articles have several images throughout. This breaks up the content and is more appealing. This is not a finite rule. I have seen many great articles with only the main photo.

To add media, click the media box on the left of a paragraph to add photos, video, SlideSshare, hyperlink, or a snippet.

We are finding that by adding a video (YouTube, Vimeo) these articles are not getting as much engagement. If you're thinking about adding your video podcast or other videos, I suggest transcribing it first. Transcribe the video and create an article around the transcription. Then add the video towards the end of the article or sending a link to the video.

Having Problems Writing?

I find it difficult to dedicate a time to sit and write. Did I mention I was *allergic* to writing? So much so that I will procrastinate until I have a hard deadline and I am forced to.

Many times I find inspiration when I am in the car or talking to a client on the phone. I have the best intentions of writing down my ideas when I get home or off the phone. Most times this does not happen, and when it does I cannot remember everything.

I found a great tool that you can access on your smartphones. It's called Rev.com.

Simply open the app and start recording. Even better, when you're done you can send them the recording and they will transcribe your audio for $1 a minute.

Furthermore, they just released another tool that will transcribe your videos and audio by a computer. It's pretty good and great for those short recordings. Temi.com can also be accessed by your smartphone. Within 10 minutes your recording is ready to edit and it only costs .10c a minute!

Call to Action

Want to grow your list and get hot leads? If you said yes, then you MUST have a CTA (call to action) in your article. I know it sounds elementary but you have to direct the reader what to do next. Send them to your calendar link, an optin page to get your free offer, a webinar, an event, etc.

Additionally, you should tell them to comment, like, and share your article. This helps with engagement and possible virality.

Example:

Call to Action:

1. **Get the cheatsheet here** [add your link or hyperlink to your optin page]
2. **Like and Share this article on LinkedIn:** sharing quality content increases your visibility and credibility with your followers and connections, creating conversations and potentially new business.
3. **Leave a comment below:** Let's start a conversations about [add here whatever your article was about]. I respond to all comments.

Bio

Eventhough you are the author of the article, you should still add your bio and a different CTA than above. Many times your article shows up in your extended networks' (2nd and 3rd degree connections) news feed. They don't know you yet, so by adding your photo and a short bio will encourage them to engage with you and view your profile.

Step 4: Promotion

I'm Ready To Publish - Now What?

This is something that so many people mess up, it just had to be on my list of steps. The big problem for most people is that they hit "publish," and that's it. They don't do anything else. They just throw the article out there and hope for the best. That's a big mistake. First of all, there's a reason there's a call to action at the bottom of the article. It's not a *"build it and they will come"* strategy. I refer to that as *hope marketing.*

You build value, expertise, and solutions in your published article, then you need to cross promote it. Of course, there's a lot more on this subject than I can go into, but you need to have a plan for how you're going to promote, and you need to have a system in place. Again, this is not "rocket science," but since you cannot guarantee LinkedIn will pick up every published article and promote you, you can't ignore it either. You build value in your published article, and then you must promote.

My colleague and friend, Bob Lovely, has an executive coaching business—something that could easily be viewed as a commodity. When you are selling a commodity, consumers tend to "price shop" looking for the lowest price for they can find. Bob repositioned his profile and started publishing consistently, every

Tuesday at 7 a.m. since June 2014, something his competitors don't do. Suddenly he became a "category of one" which made it impossible for his coaching prospects to "price shop" therefore making price irrelevant to his ideal client.

Bob does not have a smartphone, a website, or any fancy software. He uses Gmail and the power of LinkedIn only. He is netting six figures annually working part time. Do you want to know more? Find my case study with Bob in my bonus chapter.

What's The Best Day to Publish?

What's the best day of the week and time to post? Short answer, there is no day or time that's perfect. It's what's perfect for your audience. It's something that you will have to test and track over time.

However, I have found, as have some of my colleagues and clients, that the best days of the week that have the most engagements are Tuesday, Wednesday, or Thursday. The best times for your time zone are typically before the workday, around 6 or 7 AM, around noon, and late afternoon.

I do have a friend who finds that posting on Sunday afternoon does the best for her. That's when her audience is online the most.

How Often Should You Publish?

In the beginning when there weren't as many articles being published, weekly posts were common and encouraged. Today, with over 150,000 posts per week, LinkedIn recommends monthly but not more than~~that~~ bi-weekly.

Thinking you want to publish more often? It's a big commitment to make. It doesn't leave time for your network to digest and share your article. I recommend starting out with once a month. Get accustomed to writing and how long it's going to take you. Then, gradually move up to bi-weekly. That's 26 articles per year.

Get Ready To Promote!

Once you have clicked *Publish*, you'll want to create a short and compelling description and a few hashtags. You can add hashtags to the commentary about your article before you publish. Adding hashtags helps surface your article to members who may find it relevant.

According to LinkedIn Help, here are some tips for maximum advantage:

1. Include the hashtag symbol "#" before a relevant keyword or phrase.
2. Eliminate spaces and punctuation in each hashtag.

3. There are no limits to the number of hashtags that can be added to each article, but you should choose your hashtags wisely, so they reach the most suitable members for that article.

4. Type a hashtag in the LinkedIn homepage search bar to discover content based on your interests. For example: #OutofOffice

5. Editing your public profile settings to **Make my public profile visible to everyone** will enable anyone who searches for that hashtag to find your article.

6. You cannot edit or remove hashtags from your article once it's published. However, you can make edits to your article.

Comments & Likes

Once your article is published a portion of your network will get notified in the news feed. Once you start to get engagement, LinkedIn will notify you in the *Notifications* tab. Best practice is to respond to all comments, on your post and the article. This is a great place to get the conversation started and improve your opportunity for increased visibility.

You will also get notified when people like your article. Whether they are first, second, or third connections, this is an opportunity for you to reach out to them and start a conversation.

Email List

Most of us in business today have some sort of list. This could be in a CRM, an autoresponder, such as Constant Contact or Mailchimp, or even a list in Gmail.

Once your article is published add your article link in your e-newsletter or use a service such as Mailshake to send drip emails to your list in Gmail.

Share in LinkedIn

Immediately after you publish, make it a point to start sharing across your network in LinkedIn.

Here are some places to share:
- **Company Page**- Post your article on your company page. Make sure your employees engage with the post and share to their network.
- **Groups**- Share amongst your groups. Make sure that the article is relevant to those groups. If your content is too promotional, it might get flagged. Make sure the article is full of value.
- **First Connections**- Take time to segment and tag your connections in Sales Navigator. When you write an article that is relevant to that list, send them a personalized message with a link to your article.

Social Media

Share your article amongst all your other social media. This could include Facebook (groups, page, profile), Twitter, Instagram, Reddit, Quora, Pinterest.

A great way to share among several at a time is use a scheduling service such as Hootsuite or Buffer.

Other ideas

You may not want or need to do all of these below or above. Here are a few more ideas you may want to try.

1. Ask your friends, family, co-workers to give it a boost.
2. Use a sponsored update from your company page to boost the article.
3. Ask colleagues to re-tweet from Twitter.
4. Repurpose on your blog with a link redirecting them back to the original article.
5. Share on your news feed a couple times over the next few weeks.
6. Re-share older publisher articles (assuming they are still relevant).

Step 5: Profit

In the previous chapters I laid out a plan to position, prepare, publish, and promote. It seems like a daunting task, and it can be if you don't take the time to create your system. Once your system is in place and you have a plan to implement this will become easier to start profiting. Consistency is key here. Trust me, I don't always drink my own Kool Aid, but I know the system and can turn on a campaign and profit.

If you're a one man show, this may be a bit more challenging for you, but attainable. If you have a team, this will be much simpler. In the rest of this chapter are some ideas to help you automate and profit regardless if have a business of one or many.

Where Can I Add Automation?

For most of us, it's difficult to sit down and write. You're busy; I get it. Or, you're not a writer or you don't perceive that you are one. In an earlier chapter I briefly mentioned outsourcing your content. I also warned that if you do, you or your team MUST be part of the process. By this I mean the hard work—your research—should be done first.

Set up an editorial calendar (see topic chapter) and spend time looking for an industry expert to write for you, in your or your company's style. You should be willing to pay $40 to $200+ per article.

A couple_of_ great places to find good writers are Upwork or iWriter. My favorite is **Zerys.com**. The owner is a journalist herself and they have a network of 60k writers. This can seem daunting picking out one, but their programs range from DIY to white glove service. They have everything you need to plan, produce, polish, and publish amazing content your readers will love. It's a bit pricey, but it can be the difference of a mediocre article and one that knocks it out of the park.

Automating Social Activities

As I mentioned in the last chapter, using scheduling software such as Hootsuite and Buffer can quickly promote your article ~~quickly and~~ everywhere. Also, there are manual tasks to accomplish as well, such as responding to comments or likes, sending messages to first connections, setting up your newsletter, etc.

How To Do None Of The Work

But what if you don't want to prepare, set up, or push play, and follow up on your promotion?

Leveraging others to do these mundane tasks will allow you or your sales team to concentrate on the leads coming in.

Here are some ideas for outsourcing:

1. **Upwork**- You can find all sorts of people to do these tasks for you. The prices vary greatly and you can pay by the job or time worked.

2. **HireMyMom.com**- When I first started in my business I got paid to do small marketing projects. Expect to pay anywhere from $10 to $25 per hour depending on your project.

3. **Get a Virtual Assistant**- You can find great ones in the Philippines on your own. I recommend Daven Michael's program, 123 Employee. You have no overhead, pay monthly, get a price break for hiring a VA for more hours, and they use U.S. based phone numbers.

4. **Get an Intern**- Many colleges are looking for employers with internship opportunities. Look for interns in business or marketing programs. They may be paid or unpaid. You decide.

5. **Hire Your Kid**- Did you know you get tax advantages for hiring your own flesh and blood? That's what my CPA tells me anyway (check with your accountant). I just hired my 14 year old to run a campaign for me. He gets a job working at my kitchen table, I get to spend more time with him. It's a Win-Win!

Those are the 5 Steps to publishing with LinkedIn Publisher. Follow those steps, and you will be on your way to profitability.

But wait, there's more to this book! Keep reading through the next couple of chapters. As of this rewrite I decided to add a chapter on the very popular *short form* posts and some other bonus material.

Bonus Step:
Short form publishing (News Feed Posts)

As of this past Summer, the news feed got an algorithm makeover. For some it's been instrumental in bringing in new business, for most, they are struggling to get their posts seen.

A few years ago Facebook changed their algorithm for business pages. They were only sharing posts to about 2.5% of your fans. LinkedIn is following suit. Once you post, LinkedIn is showing your post to a fraction of your first degree network and followers. It doesn't matter if you have 500 connections or 30,000.

LinkedIn is favoring posts that get a lot of engagement within a short amount of time. If the post seems to be getting great interaction they will manually override the algorithm and open up your post to your first degree network, followers, and extended network. This is what is making it possible for posts to go viral.

In February 2015 I posted a warning about fake LinkedIn profiles. I took a snapshot of the profiles wanting to connect with me and a wrote a 600 character post. In 24 hours that post generated over 2700 likes and 768+ comments. I received 200+ connection requests, and 3 new clients (seems to be the magic number for me). It took me 10 minutes to write the post. Why did it go viral? I got clear on my target market and knew what they wanted. I didn't have to "game" the system, like people are today.

A lot has changed since 2015. LinkedIn now favors posts with native video and those broetry, or poetry type posts. How did this happen? I don't think it was by purposeful design, but a few growth hackers that figured out the algorithm and took advantage of it. LinkedIn is aware of the trend and is encouraging it, shamefully. For now, these posts are still popular. I don't know how long this trend will last, but I am going to give you an inherent advantage today.

Josh Fechter is considered by some to be the trendsetter for these "broetry" posts. He first started writing on Quora, figured out what his audience wanted, then took it to LinkedIn. In 2017 LinkedIn extended its once 600 character post to 1300 characters. This opened up the platform for those to write short stories. Josh started posting these short stories without links in the description and no photo attached. He then had his "tribe" or "pod" like the post within 30 minutes of posting. This opened it up to his extended network. He also didn't post daily. He found out that by only posting a couple times a week allowed for the post to circulate and gain virality. This allowed him to grow his network from only 2,000 or so connections to now over 56k followers, and 150 million views.

So how can you capitalize on this trend?

I could probably write an entire book on how to do this, and then it would be obsolete in a few months. I am going to give you some of my best tips in a minute. Before I do, I must tell you this. **You don't need to go viral to get new business.** *Views on LinkedIn posts hold ABSOLUTELY NO value* unless it's targeted and outcome driven.

I tested Josh's system. I did not have a pod or tribe, and my posts are only getting 14-80 or so likes and up to 14,000 views. Each one of them has translated into a new client, sparked conversations, and are keeping me "front of mind" with my network. Trust me, not everyone is going to engage, but they are watching. I have had people a year later send me a message and tell me they have been following me and consuming my content. And, because I resonated with them, and only when they were ready did they contact me.

Broetry Posts

- Write one or two line sentences. Refrain from chunky paragraphs.
- LinkedIn only shows the first two lines- the goal is to get your audience to click the *see more*
- Start your post with pain then a career relevance, or a major business change then explain it with controversy, or start with controversy and more controversy (see examples below)
- Make your post tangible. The more tangible, the more engaging.
- Write up to 1300 characters.

- Put your link in the first comment. Tell your audience in the post that the link is in the first comment.
- Use hashtags so your post can get found organically. Try creating your own hashtag to create a following. Example: Gary Vaynerchuk #askgaryv
- @mention to gain more visibility
- Try only posting Tuesday through Thursday in the timezone of your network. Best times are 10am -12pm, or 4pm - 6pm. Test this as with anything else.
- Create a tribe or pod and get your posts the initial engagement boosts. Reciprocate with each others' posts. Shares are worth 3 pts., Comments 2 pts., and Likes 1 pt.
- Have a CTA
- Keep a spreadsheet of all your posts and the activity. LinkedIn only shows the past 30 days of analytics of your posts, but they still live online. Grab snapshots, the link, and the views/likes/comments/shares. Use this data to create more posts that resonate with your audience.

Josh's Broetry Examples:

1. You can sleep in; You can't stop reading
2. My co-founder convinced me to move to L.A. to start a media agency; It took him 3 hours and couple beers to win me over
3. My boss left me after day one; Several weeks later I received an email, "We're letting you go"

Tracy's Most Popular Broetry Examples:

1. Some days…; I wake up and don't want to get out of bed
2. LinkedIn saved my life; In 2015 I sustained 3rd degree burns
3. I almost called @Darcy Juarez at GKIC and told her to cancel my spot; I was nervous as it was my first time ever speaking at an event of this caliber.
4. I write this today with the utmost gratefulness and love. ☺; 3 years ago this book on September 20th, my 45th birthday (in the photo)
5. Hard work pays off; I haven't had a vacation with my kids in 5 years.

Native Video

Native video is also getting a lot of attention and engagement. LinkedIn rolled this out in late Spring 2017. You can access this through your mobile and desktop. Although this is not live video (I think it's coming soon!), you can video live, then upload to LinkedIn news feed or post a pre-recorded video. I have done a few and they work great! I should do more but I don't like being in front of the camera. If you decide to add a description, and you should, most of the rules above apply~~apply above~~.

Here are some tips:

- Write a description about the contents of the video.

97

- You get 1300 characters, make them count.
- Use a stabilizer such as a tripod or selfie stick.
- Make sure you have good lighting and sound. Try using a lavalier microphone for better sound quality
- Brainstorm ideas before taping.
- Video up to 10 minutes. The best engagement is under 5 minutes.
- Be vulnerable, honest, real, and interesting.
- If you have link, put it in the first comment.

Ways to use video:

- Events you're attending
- 10x10 formula
- Events you're hosting
- Testimonials
- Interviews
- Company Culture
- Showcase a favorite client
- Case Studies
- Family time - try tying it in with some sort of business lesson.

Have fun with creating these posts. You don't need to become an expert copywriter or videographer. Not every post will perform well, and that's okay. The goal is for you to have activity, stay front of mind. Don't put your eggs all in one marketing basket. There are plenty of other business development activities in LinkedIn that will net far better results.

Bonus: Get a Mentor

I couldn't possibly include everything about publishing and how to be successful using articles in this book, so this is the last step of the book, and it's probably going to be the toughest one to actually follow through on. Nevertheless, if you can pull this off, then you are on the short path to publishing success. If you can find a mentor, someone that can show you the ropes in your writing, well, that's the ticket.

As I mentioned above, you don't want to reinvent the wheel. You want to be able to leverage all the great publishing talent and skills that have come before you. The easiest way is to learn from someone else who has been there and already made the mistakes and figured the important lessons out. That being said, it can be difficult to find someone who will show you the ropes, give you the shortcuts, and help you avoid the mistakes. You want someone who has been down that road and already made those mistakes for you.

I have a feeling right now that I might have lost a few friends with this book. I hope not. You see, most of those guru publishers are actually pretty nice folks, and some of them are friends of mine. I just think they tend to get caught up in their own image. Maybe they start believing their own PR. Hopefully they understand where I'm coming from with this book, and I won't lose too many friends.

Obviously, this book is more an expose than an end-to-end guide. My goal is to open your eyes and clear up a lot of the misconceptions about LinkedIn publishing. In the coming months, I will be releasing more information about my *LinkedIn to Publishing* online course. It was the responses to my final product survey for the course that prompted this book. This course will be unlike anything else that has been seen in the world of publishing training. It is structured with lessons, video, handouts, and case studies. It takes my entire publishing formula and systematizes it into discrete, easy to digest steps.

The courses aren't quite ready yet, but they will be soon. If you are on my Prime notification list, or you have opted in to one of my bonuses here in this book, then I will be sending you details as they get finalized, and you will also get a shot at the very best deal. That's it for now. Now it's time for you to go get to work on some publisher content that sells.

To Your Publishing Success,

Tracy Enos, your LinkedIn Expert and Coach

P.S. I forgot to tell you. Remember this is not "black magic." Once you get the basics of publishing down, then you can literally write your own check for your business success!

P.P.S. If you are not on my list or opted into one of the bonuses, email tracy@tracyenos.com for early notifications and questions.

Bonus: Bob Lovely Case Study

I met Bob on LinkedIn in November 2012. We connected and set up an appointment to have lunch at Applebee's a week or so later. It was a great meeting and he invited me to join him and his networking group once per week. This is how I started generating new business. Going to these networking groups weekly. They were time consuming, expensive (Couldn't pass up a glass of wine, or 3!), and most of them netted zero business. Except for Bob's group.

Bob is a trusted advisor here in Kansas City. People listen to him. He never refers people for the sake of referring. He is careful in who he makes introductions to.

In a previous chapter I mentioned how Bob has been consistently publishing on LinkedIn since June 2014. He was laid off the prior May from a corporate executive position. Knowing that he was a great speaker and eloquent with his words, I encouraged him to take advantage of LinkedIn's newest feature.

You see, Bob doesn't have any of these things:

- A website
- A fancy landing page or opt-in
- An e-book or guide to give away
- A smartphone
- A webcam on his Mac

What he has:
- Expertise
- Gmail
- A LinkedIn account
- Only 1800+ connections
- Consistency
- A deep understanding of his target audience

I giggle at these facts and love to share his story often. About a year into his publishing I suggested he "step up his game and go to the next level." He declined my suggestion. Bob is comfortable make his six figures part time.

As of April 2017, Bob fell ill. It was pretty serious and he is still recovering. He has not published since then. He told me had he kept up with the Tuesday publishing routine, by his calculations he would be making twice as much as the prior year.

Bob has assured me that he will make good on his promise and let me conduct a case study with him.

If you wish to hear his story, email me at tracy@tracyenos.com.

In the subject line add: I want Bob's story

I will add you to the list and when his case study is ready I will send it to you.

Time to get publishing! As Tim Ferris would say, "If Bob can do it, so can YOU!"

About Tracy Enos

Tracy Enos is Kansas City's top LinkedIn Expert Advisor, Score.org volunteer, and single Mom of 4. In July of 2015 she sustained 3rd degree burns, a 6 day stint in the burn unit, and 5 surgeries in 9 months. She wrote her first article the following October. It was featured in LinkedIn Pulse, and generated five-figures in just two hours of work.

With over 19 years of skilled experience, Tracy serves a wide variety of clients including entrepreneurs, small to mid-sized companies, start-up ventures and Internet media organizations. A seasoned business and internet media coach, Tracy drives core business processes for the clients she serves including LinkedIn Training, Social Media, Book Marketing and Public and Media Relations.

In the last 6 years Tracy has consulted 1000's of business owners, SaaS companies, coaches, authors, service professionals, sales teams and entrepreneurs how to use LinkedIn to generate leads, become the authority in their industry and stay front of mind with their clients.

She is known globally for her LinkedIn knowledge and training with clients in the U.S., Canada, Australia, Israel, and the U.K.

Her consulting expertise has netted her clients speaking engagements, media attention, guest articles in major publications and trade magazines, and millions of dollars in new business.

Book Tracy to Speak

Need a dynamic speaker or want to learn how to generate consistent leads with LinkedIn? Call Tracy at (816) 607-1570 or email her tracy@tracyenos.com

She can be reached at her personal website at:
www.TracyEnos.com

LinkedIn: www.linkedin.com/in/tracyenos

Facebook (Fan Page): www.facebook.com/TracyEnosKC/

About Michael Kravets, Editor

Michael Kravets is an educator, writer, editor, writing instructor, and content creator. After obtaining a Master of Arts in English and a Kansas Teaching License, he spent 23 years in public K-14 education as a teacher, writing instructor, technology policy writer, technology trainer, and, ultimately, Director of Technical Services for a northeast Kansas school district. As Director, Michael often used his writing and editing skills to create reports, policy documents, web content, training materials, newsletter content, and curriculum documents.

In 2013 Michael left public education to found, with his wife Lori, MTK Consulting, LLC. The focus of MTK Consulting is to provide small businesses and nonprofits with writing, editing, grant writing, and training in all aspects of communication with their customers, clients, and partners.

In addition to MTK Consulting, Michael also serves as Executive Editor of Executive Life Magazine. You can see examples of his writing and editing at http://enjoyexecutivelife.com/

Michael strongly believes that every writer needs a good editor. A good editor stands in for your readers and helps you see your work

106

from their perspective. The partnership forged between author and editor

- helps the author more easily reach his or her readers
- encourages the author to grow beyond his or her comfort zone
- shows the author how to be the best writer he or she can be.

Michael is ready to help you with your book-length project, or any other writing project you may have.

Please contact him via email: michael@mtkconsulting.com and mention *LinkedIn Publishing To Profits* when you do.

Visit his website: http://mtkconsulting.com/editorialservices/

LinkedIn: https://www.linkedin.com/in/mkravets/

Made in the USA
Middletown, DE
10 October 2018